CA Proficiency

TAXATION 1 (NI) Toolkit

2016–2017

Published in 2016 by
Chartered Accountants Ireland
Chartered Accountants House
47–49 Pearse Street
Dublin 2
www.charteredaccountants.ie

© The Institute of Chartered Accountants in Ireland, 2016

This publication is designed to provide accurate and authoritative information in regard to the subject matter covered. It is provided on the understanding that the Institute of Chartered Accountants in Ireland is not engaged in rendering professional services. The Institute of Chartered Accountants in Ireland disclaims all liability for any reliance placed on the information contained within this publication and recommends that if professional advice or other expert assistance is required, the services of a competent professional should be sought.

ISBN: 978-1-910374-55-9

Typeset by Deanta Global Publishing Services
Printed by eprint, Dublin

Contents

Introduction

As part of the CA Proficiency 1 course, you will take on the role of 'Chris', a fictitious trainee chartered accountant. Chris's job entails specific responsibilities for three clients, detailed on the following pages. As you work through the material in each of the subject areas, you will be asked to attempt tasks presented to Chris on behalf of each of these clients. These tasks are designed to help you apply the knowledge and skills required for your professional examinations.

You should treat these simulations as though they are real-life tasks. Try and put yourself in Chris's position – considering how you might respond to the client, where you might go to get information and when you might ask for help. While some of the tasks will be completed within the lecture setting, others will be available for you to complete in your own time. Watch out for the signposts on these tasks: often they will refer you to some necessary pre-reading. The signposts will also note where you can find supplementary questions.

Chris's Background

You are Chris, a trainee accountant with Shield Kenwick, Chartered Accountants & Registered Auditors. Your manager is one of the partners, Mr Ryan. You have just received the following memo from him.

SHIELD KENWICK
CHARTERED ACCOUNTANTS &
REGISTERED AUDITORS

INTERNAL MEMO

To: Chris
From: Mr Ryan
Re: Update following six-month review meeting

At your recent review meeting we agreed that you are ready to take on some extra responsibility and that you should have further direct exposure to clients. I have considered how this might be best achieved, and have decided the following:

Jane Dough – The Dough House

Jane Dough is a new client, starting up a new business. As part of your duties you will be the first point of contact and reference for any queries from Jane. In particular, you will be responsible for the preparation of Jane's books and records, income tax, PAYE and VAT returns. These will be signed off by me in the usual way. I have included background notes on Jane in **Appendix 1**.

My Company Limited (MCL)

As part of your duties, you have been seconded one day per week as assistant management accountant to a busy manufacturing company that is a client of the firm. Shield Kenwick provides general support and advice, along with accounting and taxation services, to this client. We do not carry out the statutory audit. The company, My Company Limited (MCL), is family-owned and you will report directly to the Finance Director, Mike Smithers, while at the office. Additionally, I hope that you will come directly to me with any specific queries you would like to discuss. I have included some basic background information on MCL in **Appendix 2**.

I anticipate that these responsibilities should help to address some of the areas of concern we had in relation to the competencies identified in the Online CA Diary. I suggest we keep the process under review over the next six to 12 months.

Having agreed to Mr Ryan's suggestions, you return to your desk and continue work.

Appendix 1: Jane Dough – The Dough House

On 1 January 2016, Jane Dough established a new business, a coffee and pastry shop called 'The Dough House'. In the future, Jane hopes to also sell local pottery and produce on a small scale. Jane had identified suitable premises in a busy part of town that did not appear to be particularly well serviced by coffee and pastry shops. While Jane has extensive experience working in a coffee shop environment, having been assistant manager in a similar shop for several years, she has never owned or run her own business before.

On 1 January 2016, Jane withdrew £5,000 from her own savings and her husband John's great-aunt gave her £10,000 as a gift to put towards opening The Dough House. Jane opened a separate bank account for The Dough House, lodging £14,500 to the account and retaining £500 as petty cash. Jane then signed the deeds on The Dough House's new premises, which were for sale at £50,000, drew down a mortgage with a local building society for £45,000 and paid the balance due for the premises from the business's new bank account. The mortgage is repayable over 20 years and the repayments, which are due at the end of each month, are fixed at £250 per month.

While Jane had taken redundancy from her previous employer, the redundancy payment is not expected for some months due to circumstances outside her control.

Jane will need help at lunchtime and weekends in The Dough House, and her nephew and niece have agreed to help, as long as they are paid in cash; they are 14 and 17 years old, respectively. Additionally, Jane's husband, John, has agreed to help whenever possible. Jane is uncertain whether or not she needs to register as an employer.

Jane and John have two young children, and her husband's incapacitated great-aunt lives with them. John is not employed as he cares for their two children on a full-time basis at home. However, he does have an interest in some rental properties and a small share portfolio. Jane and John have always tried to save a percentage of their income and these savings are kept in a variety of accounts: Credit Union Account, Deposit Account and ISAs. In addition, Jane and John each have a personal pension, life assurance (with critical illness) and permanent health insurance (PHI).

Appendix 2: My Company Limited (MCL)

MCL is a large, privately owned company. It was founded in the 1970s by Matthew Smithers and is still owned by the Smithers family. There has been no change in the ordinary share capital of the company for a number of years and the shareholdings are as follows:

Member	Role	Current Shareholding
Matthew and Maureen Smithers	Founders	8%
Matthew Jnr	CEO	22%
Michael	Finance Director	22%
Martina	Production Director	22%
Millie	Sales and Marketing Director	22%
Mervin (based in New York)	Not involved in the company	4%

Matthew Jnr, Michael, Martina and Millie are the only children of Matthew and Maureen. There are no other directors.

MCL is a textiles company that is involved in producing standard fabric dyes and weaving natural fibre fabrics for use in a variety of home furnishings. The dyes produced are used to dye yarns in-house (but could also be sold directly to third parties). The majority of the woven fabrics are sold in the UK and mainland Europe. There is also a core Irish market.

MCL has a large workforce, which includes: general operatives; weavers (general and skilled); stores team; administration team; and sales and distribution team. Although the company has performed well in the past, it has come under increasing pressure in the last two years.

Jane Dough – Sole Trader

Meeting 1: 4 January 2016

Jane Dough has asked you to explain what her responsibilities are in relation to income tax, PAYE/NIC and VAT. Before you go back to advise Jane, you speak with Mr Ryan, who gives you the following pointers.

1. Obligations under PAYE/NIC

You must register as an employer with HMRC once you start employing someone, or have taken on subcontractors, and:

- the employee already has another job;
- he or she is receiving a state, company or occupational pension;
- his or her earnings are equal to or above the PAYE threshold and are liable for deductions of tax;
- his or her earnings are equal to or above the National Insurance lower earning limit; or
- you are providing the employee with benefits in kind.

You can register up to 120 days in advance of the first payday. New employers can apply to register by using HMRC's online tax registration system.

If the employer received a **Form P45** from the new employee, then the new employer will fill in details of the new employment using the information from the P45.

The new employer can now operate PAYE on a cumulative basis in respect of the new employee (provided the PAYE code on the P45 is not a Month 1 code). Jane will operate under the Real Time

Information (RTI) PAYE system and report all starter and leaver information using her payroll software each time she pays an employee (via a Full Payment Submission (FPS)).

If the employee does not have a P45, the employer must ask the employee to declare their employment situation when they join. The new employee must declare which one of the following applies to their situation.

A. This is their first job since last 6 April and they have not been receiving taxable Jobseeker's Allowance, Employment and Support Allowance, taxable Incapacity Benefit, state pension, company pension or occupational pension. In this case the employer will be able to deduct tax on a cumulative basis. This means the employee will get the benefit of the personal allowance from the beginning of the tax year.
B. This is their only job, but since last 6 April they have had another job, or have received taxable Jobseeker's Allowance, Employment and Support Allowance or taxable Incapacity Benefit. In addition, they do not receive state, company or occupational pension. In this case the employer will operate an "emergency code", which operates on a non-cumulative basis. This means that the employee will be given a proportion of the normal personal allowance as his tax-free amount.
C. They have another job or receive a state, company or occupational pension. In this case the employer will use code BR. This means that tax will be deducted from the employee's pay at the basic rate (i.e. 20%) without any personal allowances being given.

Jane would be required to keep a written record of the employee's answers and report this information to HMRC on her FPS. HMRC has a "Starter Checklist" that can be used to record this information.

The exact code to be used will be determined by the declaration provided by the employee.

2. Obligations under VAT

The Dough House's core business is the supply of goods liable at the standard rate of VAT (20%). Jane is obliged to register for UK VAT once her taxable supplies exceed the £83,000 registration threshold. A voluntary registration is also possible for supplies below this threshold. It is assumed that Jane voluntarily registers for VAT on the first day of trading. Jane will be obliged to charge VAT of 20% on all food and drink supplied in catering. The hot food taken away will be standard-rated as a process has been applied to it (excluding those foods that are "naturally cooling" and are not being kept warm). Cold takeaway food is zero-rated (0%). Jane will be entitled to an input credit for any VAT incurred on food purchases, though the majority of the food purchased will be zero-rated. Thus Jane will most likely be in a VAT-payable position at the end of each three-month VAT period.

A VAT-registered trader must keep full records of all transactions that affect their liability to VAT. The records must be kept up-to-date and be sufficiently detailed to enable a trader to accurately calculate liability or repayment, and to enable HMRC to check the calculations, if necessary.

The records should show the date of the purchase invoice and a consecutive number (in the order in which the invoices are filed), the name of the supplier, the cost exclusive of VAT and the applicable rate of VAT. Purchases at each rate must be recorded separately. The same information should be recorded in respect of imports, intra-EU acquisitions and services received.

The sales records must include the amount charged in respect of every sale to a registered person and a daily entry of the total amount charged in respect of sales to unregistered persons, distinguishing in all cases between transactions liable at each different VAT rate (including the zero rate) and exempt transactions. All such entries should be cross-referenced to relevant invoices, sales dockets, cash register tally rolls, delivery notes, etc. Traders who are authorised to account for VAT on the basis of monies received (cash receipts basis) are also obliged to retain all documents they use for the purposes of their business.

Persons involved in intra-EU acquisitions also have requirements in relation to the retention of records as regards certain transfers of goods to other Member States. A taxable person must retain all books, records and documents relevant to the business, including invoices, credit and debit notes, receipts, accounts, cash register tally rolls, vouchers, EC Sales Lists (ESLs) and Intrastat returns, stamped copies of customs entries and other import documents and bank statements.

These business records must be retained for six years from the date of the latest transaction to which they refer, unless written permission from HMRC has been obtained for their retention for a shorter period.

A VAT-registered person normally accounts for VAT on a three-monthly basis (not necessarily calendar quarter dates). Traders can, in essence, choose any dates to suit their particular entity, subject to obtaining agreement from HMRC.

It is compulsory to submit VAT returns online and pay any VAT due electronically. It would be advisable for Jane to register online so that she can submit her VAT returns electronically. VAT returns submitted online must be filed, and any VAT due paid, within one month and seven days of the end of the relevant quarter. Therefore, the VAT return for the quarter ended 31 March 2016 would not be due until 7 May 2016.

3. Income tax obligations

As a self-employed person, Jane becomes a "chargeable person" for the purposes of self-assessment income tax. She must also file a tax return for each tax year. Tax returns are issued in April each year to those taxpayers who have filed returns in previous years, or notified HMRC that they need a return.

If a taxpayer wishes to file a paper return, it must be submitted by the filing date, which is the later of:

- 31 October following the tax year; or
- three months after it is issued.

However, taxpayers also have the option of filing income tax returns online. An online return must be submitted by 31 January following the tax year. Where no return is issued and an individual is chargeable to tax, they must notify HMRC within six months of the end of the tax year in which they became chargeable. Failure to do so will result in a penalty. The maximum penalty for failure is the amount to which the taxpayer is assessed for that year, which is not paid by the next 31 January following that tax year. The taxpayer can amend the tax return within 12 months after the filing date.

Meeting 2: 29 January 2016

Jane has completed her first month in business and is registered for PAYE/NIC and VAT. She has received what she calls a 'mountain' of information from HMRC on both VAT and PAYE/NIC. Jane employed Donna Moss as a part-time assistant and agreed with her a gross hourly wage of £10. Donna has provided a P45 from her previous employer. Jane has asked for your help in calculating what she owes Donna for her first week's wages, which ended on 29 January. Donna worked 23 hours in that week.

The following amounts are taken from Donna's P45:

Tax code (2015/16):	1060L
Total pay to date:	£9,640
Total tax deducted:	£215.66

Task 1

Calculate Donna's first week's wages using a temporary tax deduction card, as described above.

Jane has been approached by a couple of local businesses that want to know if she would be interested in supplying tea, coffee, soup and sandwiches for lunchtime meetings. Jane feels that this would be a great addition to her business, but is unsure of the VAT implications of same.

Task 2

Make a note of the VAT implications of this for your discussions with Jane.

Meeting 3: 1 April 2016

Jane has now completed three months' trading and the business is beginning to grow. She has also obtained a number of contracts with local companies to supply food for lunchtime meetings. Jane has been using an old cash till that will only give a total daily figure for food sales and beverages – it does not calculate VAT.

Jane has received confirmation that she is chargeable to VAT on a cash receipts basis.

Jane has taken on her niece, Kate Holmes, as a part-time assistant, but has not received a P45. Kate had another job in the tax year before this one, but does not yet have her P45 from the previous employment. Kate makes a declaration to this effect when starting with Jane. Jane paid Kate £105, £235 and £30 for the last three weeks of February. Donna was paid £220, £290 and £300 for the first three weeks in February.

The analysis of Jane's till receipts for the first three months are as follows:

Till Receipts	Food (incl. Coffee)	Minerals
£	£	£
7,650	6,732	918

Jane also had the following credit sales:

Customer	Total	Food	Beverages – Hot	Confectionery & Minerals	Date Paid
	£	£	£	£	
Cartwright	2,200	1,650	340	210	22/02/16
Corpus Ltd	2,500	1,575	405	520	o/s

Her purchases for the period were as follows:

Date	Supplier	Total	VAT
		£	£
04/01/2016	Country Foods	1,000.00	44.10
16/01/2016	Fine Fare	1,500.00	209.93
05/02/2016	Country Foods	1,200.00	54.60
16/02/2016	Jones Printing	750.20	113.73
28/02/2016	Bob's Builders	567.50	67.50
02/03/2016	Fine Fare	1,400.00	77.70
19/03/2016	Country Foods	3,300.00	231.00
21/03/2016	Main Supplies	487.85	58.03
TOTAL		10,205.55	856.59

Task 3

Based on the above information, calculate Jane's VAT liability for the VAT quarter 1 January–31 March 2016.

Task 4

Calculate Kate's net wages for the last three weeks of February.

Task 5

Calculate Donna's wages figures for the first three weeks of February.

Meeting 4: 4 April 2016

Having completed her first quarter, Jane is anxious to ensure that she calculates and makes payment for PAYE/NIC. Kate has still not received a tax code. She was paid £130, £95, £150 and £210 for the four weeks of March and £130 on 1 April.

Donna Moss was paid as follows for the remainder of the quarter:

	£
25/02/2016	360
04/03/2016	320
11/03/2016	380
18/03/2016	290
25/03/2016	400
01/04/2016	220

Task 6

Complete the PAYE/NIC summary for the period January–March 2016. (*Note:* in practice such a summary would be generated by the employer's software and there would be no need to maintain a paper record.)

Meeting 5: 29 April 2016

Task 7

Draft a short note for Jane describing the typical forms used by employers at the end of the tax year. Include a brief reference to how she might register for online filing.

Meeting 6: 1 July 2016

Jane wishes to complete her VAT return for the three months from April to June. During that period Jane brought two of her business customers out to dinner at a local restaurant, Isaac's, to thank them for their support. The payment for this bill is included in the purchases figure below. The amount, inclusive of standard-rated VAT, was £490. Jane's husband, John, purchased a television from MVision for £840 gross for his incapacitated aunt and wishes to claim back the VAT through the business. This amount is included in the purchases figure below. Jane purchased some kitchen equipment from a supplier called Gunter's Kitchens, in Germany, and at their request supplied them with her VAT number, though she is unsure why they wanted it. Jane was billed and paid Gunter's Kitchens £1,290. Jane also sold three of her new restaurant tables and some chairs to a friend as they were surplus to requirements.

Jane's records for the three-month period were as follows:

Purchases

Total	VAT
£	£
18,221.93	1,523.20

Analysis of cash receipts

Total	Till Receipts	*Misc. Customers	Credit**
£	£	£	£
24,400	12,420	700	11,280

* *Miscellaneous receipts: sale of furniture £700.*
** *All credit sales were paid within the quarter April–June.*

Task 8

Complete Jane's VAT3 return for the three months ending 30 June 2016.

Meeting 7: 4 July 2016

Jane's employee, Donna, left The Dough House on 1 July and Jane wants to give her a Form P45, but is unsure how to complete it.

Donna's earnings until leaving were as follows:

	£
08/04/2016	250.00
15/04/2016	320.00
22/04/2016	340.00
29/04/2016	290.00
06/05/2016	250.00
13/05/2016	200.00
20/05/2016	280.00
27/05/2016	230.00
03/06/2016	380.00
10/06/2016	100.00
17/06/2016	120.00
24/06/2016	360.00
01/07/2016	420.00

Task 9

Complete Donna's P45 and Jane's requirements under RTI in respect of Donna's leaving.

Meeting 8: 7 April 2017

Jane has now completed a full year's trading and has a set of accounts showing her net profit for the year. She wants to know what tax liability arises on these profits. She has also provided additional information concerning herself and her husband, John, and would like to know how much tax is payable for the tax year 2016/17.

Jane's profit and loss account for The Dough House for 2016 is as follows:

The Dough House Statement of Profit or Loss for the Year Ended 31 December 2016		
	£	£
Sales		89,600
Cost of sales:		
Opening inventory	–	
Purchases	56,400	
Closing inventory	(250)	(56,150)
Gross profit		33,450

Expenses:

Depreciation on premises (2% × £50,000 (Note 1))	1,000	
Depreciation on delivery van (25% × £6,000 (Note 1))	1,500	
Depreciation on fixtures and fittings (20% × £4,000 (Note 1))	800	
Bad debts (10% × £650 (Note 2))	65	
Insurance (incl. van insurance of £410)	720	
Stationery and advertising	900	
Postage and telephone	400	
Heat and light	1,030	
Staff wages	5,775	
Mortgage interest (12 × £62.50)	750	
General expenses (Note 3)	550	(13,490)
Net profit		**19,960**

Notes:

1. Depreciation:

Premises	– 2% on cost;
Delivery van	– 25% on cost; and
Fixtures and Fittings	– 20% on cost.

2. It is expected that approximately 10% of the other receivables will not be received.
3. Included in general expenses are:

	£
Customer entertainment costs	490
Profit on sale of tables and chairs (original cost £650)	(50)
Prize for local ICA raffle	30
Sundries	80
Total	550

The Dough House
Statement of Financial Position as at 31 December 2016

Assets	£	£
Non-current assets:		
Premises (£50,000 – £1,000 depreciation)		49,000
Delivery van (£6,000 – £1,500 depreciation)		4,500
Fixtures and fittings (£4,000 – £800 depreciation)		3,200
		56,700
Current assets:		
Inventory	250	
Trade receivables	1,585	
Other receivables	650	
Prepayments – insurance	60	

continued overleaf

Bank	6,100	
Cash	300	8,945
		65,645
Owner's Interest and Liabilities		
Owner's interest:		
Capital		15,000
Profit		19,960
Drawings		(16,050)
		18,910
Non-current liabilities:		
Mortgage (18 years × 12 months × (£250 – £62.50))		40,500
Current liabilities:		
Trade payables	3,905	
Accruals	80	
Mortgage (12 months × (£250 – £62.50))	2,250	6,235
		65,645

Jane also supplies you with the following personal information, which is not reflected in the accounts of The Dough House:

1. Jane's husband, John, works full time in the home caring for their two children.
2. John received £18,500 from the rental of two furnished properties owned by him. The details are as follows:

	Property A	Property B
	£	£
Rent received	10,200	8,300
Insurance (06/04/2016–05/04/2017)	1,920	850
Repairs (06/08/2016–05/04/2017)	550	320
Bank loan interest (06/04/2016–05/04/2017)	1,800	1,670
Replacement beds (purchased 2016)		830
First let	6 April 2016	6 August 2016

3. John received deposit interest of £1,625 from his Bank of Ireland (BOI) deposit account and interest of £520 from a small deposit account in the Cayman Islands. He also received a dividend of £422 from a UK company, Suas Plc.
4. John did a once-off piece of consultancy work for a local engineering firm, for which he was paid £1,500.
5. It is estimated that Jane uses The Dough House's delivery van for personal purposes approximately 20% of the time. She pays for her own diesel.
6. Jane took out a personal pension and paid £390 per month (net) for eight months in 2016/17.
7. Jane received redundancy money of £8,500 from her previous employer in July 2016 and lodged it to a bank account and received £425 interest in 2016/17.

Task 10

Calculate the tax-adjusted trading profits of The Dough House.

Task 11

Calculate the capital allowances.

Task 12

Calculate any relief for pension contributions that may be due to Jane.

Task 13

Identify John's miscellaneous income.

Task 14

Calculate the rental income.

Task 15

Calculate any savings income.

Task 16

Calculate any liability that might be due on the redundancy payment.

Task 17

Calculate the dividend income.

Task 18

Calculate any income tax due/(refundable), including any NIC liability for both Jane and John Dough for 2016/17. Personal allowances amount to £11,000 each.

Section 2

My Company Limited

Learning Objectives

By the end of Section 2, with respect to the taxation aspects of the course, you should be able to:

- understand the implications of domicile and residence on different income streams;
- identify non-taxable benefits and calculate taxable BIK amounts for inclusion in PAYE calculations;
- calculate income tax and NIC payable by company directors; and
- calculate allowable charges and deal with tax relief available on enterprise investments.

Meeting 1: 7 April 2017

While your role is mainly in the financial area, Mike Smithers has requested your assistance with a payroll matter. A new production director, Martina Smithers, has just been appointed (as of 6 April 2017). Mike gives you a copy of her letter of offer, which contains the following information.

Salary
Salary will be £70,000 (seventy thousand), paid monthly in arrears, and will be subject to annual review commencing from 1 June 2017.

Relocation Costs
The company will pay £4,000 (four thousand) towards any relocation expenses from Paris. The company apartment, located at 1 Market Crescent, will be made available to Martina rent-free.

Company Car
A company car, a 2010 Audi A4, will be provided. In accordance with the practice that prevails for all other directors, the company will not pay for fuel for private journeys.

Pension
The company operates a defined benefit pension scheme and Martina is eligible to become a member on appointment. The company contribution varies in accordance with actuarial requirements and Martina will be required to contribute 4% of her gross salary each month.

Subscriptions

The company agrees to contribute £1,200 per annum towards Martina's membership at Green Glens Golf Club. She will be expected to promote the company image by wearing the company golf uniform at all events at the club.

The company will also pay her annual subscription of £200 to the Institute of Engineers.

In addition, Mike tells you that the apartment on Market Crescent was bought for £90,000 in 2005 and is now worth £100,000. The gross annual value is £1,150.

The petrol Audi A4 was used by the previous production director and cost £35,000 when new and is now worth £25,000. As Martina is factory-based, Mike does not expect her annual mileage to exceed 10,000 miles. It has a CO_2 emission rating of 212g/km.

Task 19

Calculate the taxable monthly BIK for him and present it in such a way that he can give a copy to Martina to help her 'get to grips' with the UK tax system.

Meeting 2: 10 April 2017

Mike joins you for coffee and wonders if he could pick your brain. As part of its strategic plan, My Company Limited (MCL) is considering providing a share option scheme in order to retain certain key employees. However, the lawyers have only considered the company position in their report on the subject. He wonders if you could put something together that would explain the position on the basis that each key employee would be granted the option to purchase 10,000 shares at 20% discount on a 'guesstimated' flotation price of £5.20 in June 2019. In their report, the lawyers say that it is very unlikely that HMRC would grant approval for the share scheme, nor agree with the company's self-certification declaration that the scheme meets the requirements of a tax-advantaged scheme. You immediately seek clarification from Mr Ryan.

MEMO

To: Chris
From: Mr Ryan
Date: 10 April 2017
Re: Proposed Share Option Scheme

If the scheme does not meet the requirements of a tax-advantaged scheme, then income tax is charged on the difference between the option price paid and the market value of the shares at the date of exercise. No income tax liability arises in respect of the receipt of the option if the share option is potentially within the charge to tax upon exercise (which is the case in the scenario above).

If each key employee received 10,000 share options discounted at 20% on the flotation price and immediately sold them, the illustrative position would be as follows:

Income Tax Gain 2019	£
Market value of the shares on exercise	52,000
Less: option price paid	(41,600)
Income tax gain	10,400

Capital gains tax (CGT) is chargeable on disposal on the difference between sale proceeds and the market value at the date of exercise.

(For illustrative purposes, market value at disposal date in May 2023 of £15.70 is assumed.)

Gain for CGT 2023	£
Market value	157,000
Less: market value of the shares on exercise	(52,000)
Capital gain	105,000

The information above is a general outline of the tax treatment of share options. If you decide to continue with this project, I recommend obtaining expert advice from Jo Rodgers, a member of our Corporate Remuneration Team, who has significant experience in introducing share-ownership schemes of all types.

Tax may be saved by making use of tax-advantaged share option schemes. There is a range of tax-efficient schemes under which an employer can give employees a stake in the business, and they are detailed below.

SAYE (Save as You Earn) Option Scheme

An employer can set up a scheme under which employees can choose to make regular monthly investments into special bank or building society accounts, called sharesave accounts.

Employees can save a fixed monthly amount of between £5 and £500. The investments are made for three or five years and a tax-free bonus is added to the account by way of interest. At the withdrawal date, the employee can take the money in cash or can choose to buy ordinary shares in the employer's company. The price to be paid for the shares is fixed when the employee starts to save in the account. This option price must be at least 80% of the market value of the shares at the date the option is granted. The only tax charge is the CGT potentially payable when the shares are sold. The scheme must be open to all employees and to all full-time directors and on similar terms.

Company Share Option Plans (CSOPs)

In this situation, an employee may be granted options on shares under a CSOP. There is no income tax on either the grant of the option or on the profit arising from the exercise of the option between three and 10 years after the grant or on disposal of the shares. However, CGT will arise on the gain made when the employee eventually sells the shares on the difference between the exercise price and the sales price. The company can select employees to participate in the scheme. The market value of options that an individual can hold at any one time and retain the tax-favoured status are limited to £30,000 (valued at the date of the grant). The option price must be approximately equal to the market value of the shares at the time of the grant of the option. The income tax exemption is lost in respect of an option if it is exercised earlier than three years or later than 10 years after the grant.

Enterprise Management Incentives (EMIs)

These schemes are intended to encourage experienced people to 'take the plunge' and leave established careers in large companies for riskier jobs in similar, start-up or developing firms. No income tax or National Insurance contributions (NICs) are chargeable on either the grant or exercise of the options under the EMI scheme, provided that the exercise takes place within 10 years of the grant and the exercise price is the market value of the shares at the date of the grant.

The scheme enables options over shares worth up to £250,000 to be granted to each employee, provided that the total value of unexercised EMI options does not exceed £3 million. CGT will arise on the disposal of the shares.

Share Incentive Plans (SIPs)

In this plan, employers can give up to £3,600 of 'free shares' a year to employees with no tax or NIC liability. In addition, employees can purchase up to £1,800 worth of 'partnership shares' at any time in the year and the employers can 'match' this latter purchase in the ratio of 2:1 (i.e. they can provide £3,600 worth of matching shares).

Employers offering free shares must offer a minimum amount to each employee on similar terms. Once the shares are held for five years, there is no income tax or NIC chargeable.

Meeting 3: 17 April 2017

Mike meets you in the corridor as you arrive at the plant and reminds you to collect a folder of all the information to prepare his income tax return for 2016/17 and informs you that his personal circumstances have not changed since 2015/16. The file contains the following information:

1. P60 for 2016/17: gross pay £105,000; PAYE paid £10,420. A 4% pension contribution is deducted from this salary. BIK of £10,200 is included in P11D. Mike is a company director.
2. Note of a single pension payment of £8,000 paid (net of basic rate tax) on 1 April 2017.
3. Deposit account showing interest earned from First Trust Bank for the tax year 2016/17. Gross interest: £2,000.
4. Details from Last Chance Manufacturing Ltd re. an EIS scheme contribution of £75,000.
5. Declaration of gift aid donation – £2,000 paid net.
6. Certificate of interest paid for 2013 on a loan of £20,000, which financed purchase of 5% of the share capital of MCL – £1,200 charged.

You ascertain the following personal information from his tax file:

Mike is single, DOB 30/03/1982, lives alone and purchased an apartment for his mother some years ago. Apart from her State pension, his mother has no other income.

Task 20

Prepare Mike's income tax return, including NIC.

Meeting 4: 24 April 2017

Martina Smithers drops by your office. She tells you that she has just returned to the UK (where she was born) after spending 10 years in Paris. You ascertain that she is single, aged 35, with a two-year-old daughter Sarah who lives with her. Her partner, Paul (aged 52), visits from Dublin every weekend, as well as visiting for two weeks during the summer on holiday. Prior to 6 April 2017, they only visited the UK for two weeks in the summer each year.

Both she and Paul have accumulated a 'tidy nest egg' and don't want to suffer adversely from a taxation perspective by moving back to the UK or from any of their future actions. She is also keen to get some idea of how much tax they will pay in 2017/18. Before she launched into detail, she expressed concern about the confidentiality of the information she would provide, as she is aware that your company acts as general advisor to MCL. Your response should address this key concern first.

Martina gives you the following details of her investments:

- Verizon LLC shares in the USA, yielding an annual gross dividend of £3,750 with US dividend tax of £562.50.
- Deposit account at Banque Paribas of £300,000 from the sale of their Paris apartment. It is on a monthly deposit and at the moment she earns 4% on it. She plans to buy a home locally out of this account and has already spotted some suitable houses.
- Holiday chalet in the French Alps, which yields £11,800 net of expenses. This property is owned jointly with Paul.

Paul is a Dubliner, born and bred. He works for Merchant Bank International in Dublin and hopes to get a transfer to a Belfast branch in 2018, when they plan to marry. Meanwhile, he commutes to Dublin from where he lives with his mother in Ballsbridge from Monday to Friday. He spends Friday and Saturday nights in Belfast.

Apart from the chalet, he has a holiday home in Essex that he lets out and receives approximately £8,000 in cash from a local letting agency each year while on vacation in the UK. He has not filed a tax return in the UK since he bought the property in 2013.

He also has an Irish portfolio of investments that yields £27,000 net of Irish tax of £3,000 annually. His Irish salary is the equivalent of £55,000.

Task 21

On the basis that MCL pays a small fixed fee of £500 to prepare a basic income tax return for each director, draft a short briefing note for Martina, noting any ethical issues that may arise.

Task 22

Write a briefing note to Martina describing the basic rules around residency and domicile.

Task 23

Based on the personal and investment details supplied by Martina and using the information received from Mike on 7 April 2017 (Task 19), complete a projected income tax return for Martina for 2017/18. You may use credits/reliefs applicable for 2016/17. Include a note of her income tax return, payment and filing obligations in the UK.

> ### Task 24
>
> Likewise, complete a projected income tax return for Paul, including a note of his income tax return, payment and filing obligations.

Meeting 5: 10 January 2018

Mike has requested that you prepare the VAT return for October–December 2017 as the person who normally prepares it is out sick. You also note that the EC Sales List has not been prepared.

You print off a copy of the VAT on sales and VAT on purchases reports and start the 'long' process of reconciling them with the VAT account.

You immediately note that the VAT on sales and purchases reports do not agree with the VAT account.

- A petty cash journal for £1,074.38 + VAT of £214.88 was posted directly to the VAT account as the supplier would not accept a cheque and received cash instead. There is no invoice to support this transaction. Nothing has yet been included in the VAT on purchases report in respect of this amount.
- A direct debit to Dryers America Inc. for plant on 12 November for VAT at point of import, under the deferred payment scheme, for £3,150, was posted to the VAT account. You have the SAD and supplier invoice from Dryers America Inc. for a new fabric dryer from the USA. The SAD shows VAT of £2,900 and duty payable of £250. The total VAT amount has not been included in the VAT on purchases report.
- MCL has accounted for 20% in the VAT on purchases report and the VAT account in respect of an invoice from M. Wiley Ltd (Ireland). Another invoice was received from Weave Magic GmbH (Germany) for repairs. Nothing to date has been done with respect to VAT in relation to this invoice. The two invoices are reproduced below.
- An amount for £1,153.80 was incurred from Materials Unlimited Inc. (USA) and is included in the VAT on purchases report (19 November 2017), but VAT has not been accounted for on this report nor in the VAT account. You have received the SAD document and VAT is paid using deferred VAT direct debit.

There are only a few sales invoices in this period and their accounts system produced the EC Sales List for the quarter ended December 2017, except for two new small customers, Phillipa Treacy and Marshia Joan. Their invoices are also reproduced below.

M. Wiley **2 Main Street** **Castlecomer** **Kilkenny** **VAT No. IE12345**
My Company Ltd **Towncentre Industrial Park** **Belfast** **11 November 2017**
Purchase of fabric-cutting table   **£13,300.00** **Customer VAT No. GB81487339**
VAT @ 0%   **£13,300.00**

Weave Magic GmbH
Hamburg
Germany
VAT No. 12345678

My Company Ltd
Towncentre Industrial Park
Belfast
8 December 2017
Machine repairs   £1,050.00
Customer VAT No. GB81487339
VAT @ 0%   £1,050.00

My Company Ltd
Towncentre Industrial Park
Belfast
VAT No. GB81487339

Phillipa Treacy
Goldhawk Road
Dublin
10 December 2017
Customer VAT No. IE7264258K
Purple/White Umbrella Cloth   £300.00
VAT @ 0%   £300.00

My Company Ltd
Towncentre Industrial Park
Belfast
VAT No. GB81487339

Marshia Joan
Polder 52
Schipol Holland
07 November 2017
Candy Pink Dye   £404.93
VAT @ 0%   £404.93

VAT on Purchases October–December 2017		
Net		**VAT**
£		**£**
150,761.21		19,217.18
VAT on Sales October–December 2017		
Net		**VAT**
£		**£**
175,400.00		1,501.50

My Company Ltd – VAT Account from 1 October 2017–31 December 2017				
			DR	CR
			£	£
31/12/2017		Closing balance	21,080.46	

Task 25

Prepare the VAT return for October to December 2017, making any amendments necessary from your reconciliation. You should explain these amendments.

Task 26

Prepare a short briefing note for Mike, outlining when he might have to prepare an Intrastat return or EC Sales List.

Assume VAT rates for 2017/18 are as for 2016/17.

Solutions to Tasks

Task 1 Solution

Calculation of net wages for Donna Moss

Income tax calculation

				K codes only				K codes only			K codes only
Week number	Pay in the week or month, including statutory payments (SSP/SMP/SPP/SAP)	Total pay to date	Total 'free pay' to date	Total 'addi-tional' pay to date	Total taxable pay to date	Total tax due	Tax due at end of current period	Regu-latory limit: 50% of column 2 entry	Tax deducted or refunded in the week or month	Tax not deducted owing to regulatory limit
	2	3	4a	4b	5	6	6a	6b	7	8
42		9,640.00	8,561.70		1,078.30	215.66				
43	230.00	9,870.00	8,765.55		1,104.45	220.89			5.23	
	Gross pay			23 hours @ £10 per hour						
				= £230.00						

'Free pay' to date		Tax at basic rate band 20%	Total tax
£10,600/52 = £203.85			
£203.85 × 43 = £8,765.55	All taxed at 20% after PA	1,104.45	220.89

NIC calculation

Week number	Earnings at LEL (earnings equal or exceed LEL)	Earnings above LEL (up to and including PT)	Earnings above PT (up to and including UEL)	Total of employee's and employer's contributions – *mark minus amounts 'R'*	Employee's contributions due on all earnings above PT
	1a	1b	1c	1d	1e
43	112.00	43.00	75.00	19.21	9.00

As Jane's monthly PAYE total is likely to be less than £1,500, she can choose to pay PAYE to HMRC on a quarterly, rather than a monthly, basis. The first quarterly payment would be due on 22 April for the January–March period (assuming Jane pays electronically).

Task 2 Solution

VAT implications for the supply of takeaway tea, coffee, sandwiches, etc.
The tea, coffee and soup taken away will be standard-rated (20% VAT), as hot takeaway food and drink which is not 'naturally cooling' is treated as standard-rated. Cold takeaway food is specifically zero-rated (subject to some standard-rated exceptions, e.g. bottled water, crisps and sweets). Where Jane has obtained a specific catering contract to supply food for lunchtime meetings, these supplies should be treated as standard-rated.

Task 3 Solution

VAT on sales calculation

Sales inclusive of VAT at 20%:

Till receipts	=	£7,650
VAT @ 1/6	=	£1,275
Credit sales receipts	=	£2,200
VAT @ 1/6	=	£366.67

VAT is due on the Cartwright receipt only as Jane operates cash accounting (i.e. she only accounts for VAT on the basis of cash paid and received).

Sales summary

	Sales	Total £	VAT £	Net £
January–March 2016	Till receipts	7,650.00	1,275.00	6,375.00
January–March 2016	Credit sales receipts	2,200.00	366.60	1,833.33
Total		9,850.00	1,641.60	8,208.33

VAT return for January–March 2016

VAT on sales	=	£1,641.60	Box 1
Less: VAT on purchases	=	£(856.59)	Box 4
Net VAT payable	=	£785.08	Box 5

Task 4 Solution

Calculation of net wages for Kate Holmes

Kate will have to be taxed on the emergency basis (1060L M1) until such time as Jane receives a tax code from HMRC. Under the RTI system, Jane would report the information for Kate on the Full Payment Submission to HMRC when making the first payment. HMRC recommends that a starter checklist be kept for the employer's own records (a template of a starter checklist is available from the HMRC website). As Kate is on an emergency code, each month is treated on its own and given an equal amount of tax-free pay each month.

Therefore Kate's position is as follows:

Income tax calculation

Week number	Pay in the week or month, including statutory payments (SSP/SMP/SPP/SAP)	Total pay to date	Total 'free pay' to date	K codes only Total 'additional' pay' to date	Total taxable pay to date	Total tax due	K codes only Tax due at end of current period	Regulatory limit: 50% of column 2 entry	Tax deducted or refunded in the week or month	K codes only Tax not deducted owing to regulatory limit
	2	3	4a	4b	5	6	6a	6b	7	8
42										
43										
44										
45		105.00	203.85							
46		235.00	203.85		31.15	6.23			6.23	
47		30.00	203.85							

'Free pay'
£10,600/52 = £203.85   Emergency rate @ 20%

NIC calculation

Week number	Earnings at LEL (earnings equal or exceed LEL)	Earnings above LEL (up to and including PT)	Earnings above PT (up to and including UEL)	Total of employee's and employer's contributions – *mark minus amounts 'R'*	Employee's contributions due on all earnings above PT
	1a	1b	1c	1d	1e
45					
46	112.00	43.00	80.00	20.50	9.60
47					

Task 5 Solution

Wages – Donna Moss

Income tax calculation

								K codes only		K codes only		K codes only
Week number	Pay in the week or month, including statutory payments (SSP/SMP/ SPP/SAP)	Total pay to date	Total 'free pay' to date	Total 'additional pay' to date	Total taxable pay to date	Total tax due	Tax due at end of current period	Regulatory limit: 50% of column 2 entry	Tax deducted or re-funded in the week or month	Tax not deducted owing to regulatory limit
	2	3	4a	4b	5	6	6a	6b	7	8
42		9,640.00	8,561.70		1,078.30	215.66				
43	230.00	9,870.00	8,765.55		1,104.45	220.89			5.23	
44	220.00	10,090.00	8,969.40		1,120.60	224.12			3.23	
45	290.00	10,380.00	9,173.25		1,206.75	241.35			17.23	
46	300.00	10,680.00	9,377.10		1,302.90	260.58			19.23	

NIC calculation

Week number	Earnings at LEL (earnings equal or exceed LEL)	Earnings above LEL (up to and including PT)	Earnings above PT (up to and including UEL)	Total of employee's and employer's contributions – *mark minus amounts 'R'*	Employee's contributions due on all earnings above PT
	1a	1b	1c	1d	1e
43	112.00	43.00	75.00	19.21	9.00
44	112.00	43.00	65.00	16.63	7.80
45	112.00	43.00	135.00	34.69	16.20
46	112.00	43.00	145.00	37.27	17.40

Task 6 Solution

Calculation of PAYE/NIC Kate Holmes

Income tax calculation

Week number	Pay in the week or month, including statutory payments (SSP/SMP/ SPP/SAP)	Total pay to date	Total 'free pay' to date	K codes only Total 'addi-tional pay' to date	Total taxable pay to date	Total tax due	K codes only Tax due at end of current period	Regula-tory limit: 50% of column 2 entry	Tax de-ducted or refunded in the week or month	K codes only Tax not deducted owing to regula-tory limit
	2	3	4a	4b	5	6	6a	6b	7	8
42										
43										
44										
45	105.00		203.85							
46	235.00		203.85		31.15	6.23			6.23	
47	30.00		203.85							
48	130.00		203.85							
49	95.00		203.85							
50	150.00		203.85							
51	210.00		203.85		6.15	1.23			1.23	
52	130.00		203.85							

NIC calculation

Week number	Earnings at LEL (earnings equal or exceed LEL)	Earnings above LEL (up to and including PT)	Earnings above PT (up to and including UEL)	Total of employee's and employer's contributions – *mark minus amounts 'R'*	Employee's contributions due on all earnings above PT
	1a	1b	1c	1d	1e
45					
46	112.00	43.00	80.00	20.50	9.60
47					
48	112.00	18.00			
49					
50	112.00	38.00			
51	112.00	43.00	55.00	14.05	6.60
52	112.00	18.00			

Calculation of PAYE/NIC Donna Moss

Income tax calculation

								K codes only	K codes only	K codes only
Week number	Pay in the week or month, including statutory payments (SSP/SMP/SPP/SAP)	Total pay to date	Total 'free pay' to date	Total 'additional pay' to date	Total taxable pay to date	Total tax due	Tax due at end of current period	Regulatory limit: 50% of column 2 entry	Tax deducted or refunded in the week or month	Tax not deducted owing to regulatory limit
	2	3	4a	4b	5	6	6a	6b	7	8
42		9,640.00	8,561.70		1,078.30	215.66				
43	230.00	9,870.00	8,765.55		1,104.45	220.89			5.23	
44	220.00	10,090.00	8,969.40		1,120.75	224.12			3.23	
45	290.00	10,380.00	9,173.10		1,206.75	241.35			17.23	
46	300.00	10,680.00	9,377.10		1,302.90	260.58			19.23	
47	360.00	11,040.00	9,580.95		1,459.05	291.81			31.23	
48	320.00	11,360.00	9,784.80		1,575.35	315.04			23.23	
49	380.00	11,740.00	9,988.65		1,751.35	350.27			35.23	
50	290.00	12,030.00	10,192.50		1,837.50	367.50			17.23	
51	400.00	12,430.00	10,396.35		2,033.65	406.73			39.23	
52	220.00	12,650.00	10,600.20		2,049.80	409.96			3.23	

NIC calculation

Week number	Earnings at LEL (earnings equal or exceed LEL)	Earnings above LEL (up to and including the PT)	Earnings above PT (up to and including the UEL)	Total of employee's and employer's contributions – mark minus amounts 'R'	Employee's contributions due on all earnings above PT
	1a	1b	1c	1d	1e
43	112.00	43.00	75.00	19.21	9.00
44	112.00	43.00	65.00	16.63	7.80
45	112.00	43.00	135.00	34.69	16.20
46	112.00	43.00	145.00	37.27	17.40
47	112.00	43.00	205.00	52.75	24.60
48	112.00	43.00	165.00	42.43	19.80
49	112.00	43.00	225.00	57.91	27.00
50	112.00	43.00	135.00	34.69	16.20
51	112.00	43.00	245.00	63.07	29.40
52	112.00	43.00	65.00	16.63	7.80

PAYE/NIC Summary for the period January–March 2016

	PAYE £	NIC (employee and employer) £	Total £
Donna Moss	194.30	375.28	569.58
Kate Holmes	7.46	34.55	42.01
Total Jan–Mar 2016	**201.76**	**409.83**	**611.59**

The "employment allowance" of £3,000 for the 2015/16 tax year will be available to Jane and will reduce her Class 1 secondary NIC liability. The allowance is intended encourage business growth and to help small businesses in particular with the costs of employment. It can be claimed through the Employment Payment Summary (EPS) on RTI. In this quarter, Jane will have utilised £218.43 of the employment allowance. Therefore, the PAYE and NIC liability due for the quarter will be £611.59 − £218.43 = £393.16.

Task 7 Solution

Briefing Note
The employer must provide the employee with a **Form P60** by 31 May following the end of the tax year. Form P60 shows the employee's total taxable earnings, total tax deducted, the employee tax code, NIC number, name and address. At the end of the tax year, the employer will submit their final Full Payment Submission (FPS) for the pay period as normal – on or before the date they pay their employees.

For most employers, this means they will send their final FPS on or before their last payday in the tax year, which ends on 5 April. Employers must indicate that this is the final submission for the tax year when submitting the FPS and also answer the end-of-year questions and declaration.

To register for **online filing**, the employer will need the 'Employer PAYE reference' and 'Accounts Office reference'; these can be found on the yellow PAYE payslip booklet. The employer will create a password and, within seven days, will get a user identity (User ID) confirmation letter with a card showing the user ID, along with a letter showing their activation PIN. The employer must activate the service within 28 days of registering.

Task 8 Solution

1. VAT on purchases

VAT is not reclaimable on the customer entertainment and goods not for purposes of the trade (i.e. TV). Jane must charge herself VAT on the EU acquisition from Gunter's Kitchens and claim a simultaneous input credit, thus cancelling the liability.

Adjustments to purchases VAT analysis

Supplier	Total £	VAT £	Net £
	18,221.93	1,523.20	16,698.73
Gunter's Kitchens*		258.00	
MVision – TV	(840.00)	(140.00)	(700.00)
Isaac's Restaurant**		(82.00)	
	17,381.93	1,559.20	15,998.73

* Jane should charge herself UK VAT for the German kitchen imported and claim an input tax credit.

** Jane can keep the customer entertaining in the total and net figures as these are business expenses. As the business expense is not allowable for VAT purposes, the VAT figure should be adjusted.

Sales summary

Sales	Total £	VAT £
Till receipts	12,420.00	2,070.00
Credit sales receipts	11,280.00	1,880.00
Sale of furniture	700.00	116.67
Total	**24,400.00**	**4,066.67**
VAT on EU acquisition		
Gunter's Kitchens		258.00
Total VAT		**4,324.67**

VAT return April–June 2016

Box 1	=	£4,066.67	(VAT on Sales)
Box 2	=	£258.00	(EU Acquisitions)
Box 3	=	£4,324.67	
Box 4	=	£1,559.20	(VAT on purchases)
Box 5	=	£2,765.47	(VAT payable)

As Jane's imports from other EU Member States are unlikely to exceed the current annual exemption threshold of £1,500,000 she will not need to complete an Intrastat return.

Task 9 Solution

Income tax calculation

Week number	Pay in the week or month, including statutory payments (SSP/SMP/SPP/SAP)	Total pay to date	K codes only — Total 'free pay' to date	Total 'ad-ditional pay' to date	Total taxable pay to date	Total tax due	K codes only — Tax due at end of current period	K codes only — Regula-tory limit: 50% of column 2 entry	Tax de-ducted or refunded in the week or month	K codes only — Tax not deducted owing to regula-tory limit
	2	3	4a	4b	5	6	6a	6b	7	8
1	250.00	250.00	211.54		38.46	7.69			7.69	
2	320.00	570.00	423.08		146.92	29.38			21.70	
3	340.00	910.00	634.62		275.38	55.08			25.70	
4	290.00	1,200.00	846.16		353.84	70.77			15.69	
5	250.00	1,450.00	1,057.70		392.30	78.46			7.69	
6	200.00	1,650.00	1,269.24		380.76	76.15			2.31 R	
7	280.00	1,930.00	1,480.78		449.22	89.84			13.69	
8	230.00	2,160.00	1,692.32		467.68	93.54			3.70	
9	380.00	2,540.00	1,903.86		636.14	127.23			33.69	
10	100.00	2,640.00	2,115.40		524.60	104.92			22.31 R	
11	120.00	2,760.00	2,326.94		433.06	86.61			18.31 R	
12	360.00	3,120.00	2,538.48		581.52	116.30			29.69	
13	420.00	3,540.00	2,750.02		789.98	158.00			41.70	

Tax-free pay:
£11,000/52 = £211.54 per week

NIC calculation

Week number	Earnings at LEL (earnings equal or exceed the LEL)	Earnings above LEL (up to and including PT)	Earnings above PT (up to and including UEL)	Total of employee's and employer's contributions – *mark minus amounts 'R'*	Employee's contributions due on all earnings above PT
	1a	1b	1c	1d	1e
1	112.00	43.00	95.00	24.37	11.40
2	112.00	43.00	165.00	42.43	19.80
3	112.00	43.00	185.00	47.59	22.20
4	112.00	43.00	135.00	34.69	16.20
5	112.00	43.00	95.00	24.37	11.40
6	112.00	43.00	45.00	11.47	5.40
7	112.00	43.00	125.00	32.11	15.00
8	112.00	43.00	75.00	19.21	9.00
9	112.00	43.00	225.00	57.91	27.00
10					
11	112.00	8.00	0.00	0.00	0.00
12	112.00	43.00	205.00	52.75	24.60
13	112.00	43.00	265.00	68.23	31.80

P45 for Donna Moss

P45 extracts

1. PAYE reference

2. Employee's National Insurance number

3. Surname (in CAPITALS)   MOSS

   First name(s) (in CAPITALS)   DONNA

4. Leaving date (in figures)   01/07/2016

5. Continue student loan deductions

6. Tax code at leaving date. If Week 1 or Month 1 basis applies, write 'X' in the box marked Week 1 or Month 1.   1100L

7. Last entries on Deductions Working Sheet. Complete only if tax code is cumulative. Make no entry here if Week 1 or Month 1 basis applies.	Week or month number	13
	Total pay to date	£3,540.00
	Total tax to date	£158.00

When Donna leaves the employment, Jane must include the date of leaving on the FPS submitted when the final payment is made to Donna. In addition, Jane must give Donna her Form P45.

The P45 contains details of pay and tax from the start of the tax year to the date the employment ended. The P45 also contains the code number operated by Jane. This code number will generally be operated by Donna's new employer until a new one is issued by HMRC.

Donna will keep one part (1A) of the form for her records and will give the other parts (2 and 3) to the new employer. Under RTI, no part of the form is required to be submitted to HMRC.

Task 10 Solution

Calculation of tax-adjusted trading profits

The net profit for The Dough House for the 2016 period is not the taxable profit of the business for the year. Adjustments must be made to the profit figure for the different tax treatment of certain expenses and allowances.

The Dough House Tax-adjusted profits for the year ended 31 December 2016			
	Notes	£	£
Net profit per accounts			19,960
Add back:			
Depreciation		3,300	
General expenses – entertainment	1	490	
Bad debt provision	2	65	
Van insurance	3	82	
Prize for raffle	4	30	3,967
			23,927
Deduct:			
Profit on sale of fixed asset	5	50	(50)
Adjusted profits			**23,877**

Notes:
1. Customer entertainment – disallowed.
2. A general provision for bad debts is not allowed.
3. Personal element of insurance for van is disallowed – £410 @ 20%.
4. Charitable donations are not allowed. However, if sponsoring a prize is likely to give material advertising benefit, a strong argument could then be made to HMRC that the £30 is tax-deductible.
5. Profits on the sale of fixed assets are not taxable as trading income.

Task 11 Solution

Calculation of capital allowances

	Premises *None*	Fixtures **100%*	Delivery Van *100%*
Cost	£50,000	£4,000	£6,000
Less: AIA		(£4,000)	**(£6,000)
WDV at 31 December 2016	n/a	£0,000	£0,000

* Annual investment allowance (AIA) 100% (up to £200,000 of investment in plant and machinery, except cars, being the AIA limit in place from 1 January 2016).
** The purchase of the van will also qualify for the AIA, which will be restricted to the business use only, i.e. 80%.

Capital allowances

	£
Fixtures	4,000
Delivery van (£6,000 @ 80%)	4,800
Total capital allowances	8,800

The profit on disposal of the tables and chairs will not give rise to a balancing charge, as no capital allowances are available on assets bought and sold in the same period. As they have been sold, they will not be in the NBV at the year end in the statement of financial position. The accounts do not include any depreciation on the table and chairs, so the £50 profit on disposal gives an original cost of £650 and proceeds of £700. However, as proceeds are limited to cost for capital allowances purposes, no balancing charge arises.

Adjusted profits = £23,877 − £8,800 = £15,077

Jane will be assessed for tax year 2015/16:
1 January–5 April 2016 £15,077 × 3/12 = £3,769
Jane will be assessed for tax year 2016/17:
Year ended 31 December 2016 = £15,077
(This creates overlap profit of £3,769.)

Task 12 Solution

Relief for pension contributions
Jane is entitled to £3,900 (£390 × 100/80 × 8 months) tax relief on her contributions. She is not a higher rate tax payer (see below) and, therefore, is not entitled to further relief by extension of the basic rate band. She has already received basic rate relief by paying for contributions net of basic rate tax.

Task 13 Solution

John – miscellaneous income:
Consultancy fee of £1,500

Task 14 Solution

Calculation of rental income

	Note	Prop. A	Prop. B	Total
		£	£	£
Gross rent		10,200	8,300	18,500
Deduct:				
Insurance	1	1,920	850	2,770
Repairs		550	320	870
Loan interest	1	1,800	1,670	3,470
Replacement furniture relief			830	830
Total deductions		4,270	3,670	7,940
Rental profits		5,930	4,630	10,560

Note:
1. Property B expenses incurred before first letting are allowed in full on the basis that a property business already existed (as Property A was let from 6 April 2016).

Task 15 Solution

Calculation of savings income

John:	Deposit account Cayman Islands – Interest gross	£520
John:	BOI deposit account	£1,625
Jane:	Deposit account	£425

Task 16 Solution

Calculation of liability on redundancy payment

Jane: Redundancy payment £8,500. This is under the exemption limit of £30,000 – which should be available provided this was a bona fide redundancy payment.

Task 17 Solution

Calculation of dividend income

John: Dividend – Suas Plc   £422

Task 18 Solution

Jane Dough

Income tax computation 2016/17

	Non-savings	Savings	Total
	£	£	£
Trading income	15,077.00		15,077.00
Bank deposit interest		425.00	425.00
Net income	15,077.00	425.00	15,502.00
Less: personal allowance	(11,000)		(11,000)
Taxable income	4,077.00	425.00	4,502.00
Income tax due:			
Basic rate band: Non-savings	4,077.00	@ 20%	815.40
Basic rate band: Savings	425.00	0% (Note 1)	0.00
	4,502.00		
Tax liability/payable			815.40

Note:
1. Savings income falls within the threshold of £5,000 (starter rate for savings income) and will be taxed at 0%. The personal savings allowance of £1,000, which is available in 2016/17, is not required given the level of Jane's income.

Jane will also have a liability to NIC under Class 4 as follows:
(£15,077 − £8,060) @ 9% = £631.53

She will also pay Class 2 NIC at a rate of £145.60 per annum (£2.80 per week) during 2016/17. This will be collected in full on 31 January 2018.

John Dough

Income tax computation 2016/17

	Non-savings	Savings	Dividends	Total
	£	£	£	£
Miscellaneous income	1,500.00			1,500.00
Rental income	10,560.00			10,560.00
Bank deposit interest		1,625.00		1,625.00
Bank deposit interest – Cayman Islands		520.00		520.00
Dividends			422.00	422.00
Net income	12,060.00	2,145.00	422.00	14,627.00

continued overleaf

Less: personal allowance	(11,000.00)
Taxable income	3,627.00
Tax due at 20% on non-savings income (£1,060)	212.00
Tax due at 0% on savings income (£2,145) (Note 1)	0.00
Tax due at 0% on dividend income (Note 2)	0.00
Tax payable	(212.00)

Notes:
1. Savings income falls within the threshold of £5,000 (starter rate for savings income) and will be taxed at 0%. The personal savings allowance of £1,000, which is available in 2016/17, is not required given the level of John's income.
2. Dividend income falls within the £5,000 dividend allowance.

Task 19 Solution

MEMO

To: **Michael Smithers**

cc: **Martina Smithers**

From: **Chris, Shield Kenwick**

Date: **8 April 2017**

Re: **Taxable benefit in kind**

[Rates and allowances being used below for this example are 2016/17 rates. The 2017/18 rates may differ when published.]

As you know, in addition to salary, certain benefits received by employees are subject to the PAYE and NIC system.

Below are the calculations of Martina's gross pay per month and her benefits in kind. The tax due on the salary will be collected through the payroll. Once HMRC has been informed of Martina's benefits in kind, it will change her tax code to collect the tax due.

Total gross pay per month and benefits in kind

	£
Salary	5,833.33
Benefit in kind (Note 1)	1,337.50
Deduct: pension (Note 2)	(233.33)
Total gross pay and BIKs	6,937.50

Notes:

1. Taxable benefits:

   (a) Company car = £1,079.17 per month
       Calculation of BIK on company car is based on the original list price of the car not its current valuation.

£35,000 × 37% = £12,950 (£1,079.17 per month)

CO_2 emissions: 212g/km (rounded down to 210g/km) 210 − 95 = 115g/km

115/5 = 23%

16% + 23% = 39% but maximum is 37%

(b) Accommodation	£
GAV	1,150.00
Additional benefit	
(£100,000 – £75,000) @ 3%	750.00
	1,900.00
Per month	158.33

(c) Subscription to golf club	£100 per month (not needed for the job)
(d) Subscription to the Institute of Engineers	Nil – this would be tax-deductible in the personal tax return if paid personally by Martina
(e) Relocation expenses – allowable	Allowed up to £8,000 over two tax years provided it is "qualifying" receipted expenditure

2. Pension contribution

The company contribution to the pension scheme is not a taxable benefit. Furthermore, the amount contributed by the employee of £233.33 per month may be deducted from gross pay as full relief from PAYE is available.

Task 20 Solution

MEMO

To: **Michael Smithers**

From: **Chris, Shield Kenwick**

Date: **17 April 2017**

Re: **Income tax computation and return for 2016/17**

Based on the documents provided and information available, I have completed your income tax computation for 2016/17. The calculations of income are as follows:

Deposit account interest

	£
Gross income	2,000

Employment income

As you are a director, the amount to be included in your income tax computation is the salary per the accounts of £105,000 and benefits of £10,200.

    The deductions from your income are:

Pension

The pension contribution deducted in 2016/17 through payroll of 4% of your (paid) salary of £105,000 is calculated as follows:

Pension amount: 4% of £105,000 = £4,200

The additional pension contribution of £8,000 has already got 20% basic relief at source. Higher rate relief is available by extending the basic rate band on the grossed-up amount, i.e. £10,000 – see income tax computation.

Gift aid

The donation of £2,000 has already got 20% basic relief at source. Higher rate relief is available by extending the basic rate band on the grossed-up amount, i.e. £2,500 (£2,000 × 100/80) – see income tax computation.

Total extension of basic rate band £10,000 + £2,500 = £12,500.

Loan to invest in MCL

This will be a qualifying loan and interest can be deducted from your total income. It qualifies because:

- the company is a close company; and
- you have a material interest (greater than 5% of the equity) in the company. Even if your interest was less than 5%, it would still qualify as you satisfy the requirement of "working for the company".

Finance Act 2013 introduced a cap on, among other reliefs, qualifying loan interest, the amount of interest here is well below the permitted maximum.

Income Tax Computation 2016/17

	Non-savings £	Savings £	Total £
Employment income			
Salary	105,000		105,000
Benefits in kind	10,200		10,200
Less: pension contributions (£105,000 × 0.04)	(4,200)		(4,200)
	111,000		111,000
Bank deposit interest		2,000	2,000
Less: interest on qualifying loan	(1,200)		(1,200)
Net income	109,800	2,000	111,800
Less: personal allowance (Note 1)	(11,000)		(11,000)
Taxable income	98,800	2,000	100,800

		£	£
Income tax due:			
Basic rate band: Non-savings to £32,000	32,000 @ 20%		6,400
Extended basic rate band:	12,500 @ 20%		2,500
Higher rate band: Non-Savings	54,300 @ 40%		21,720
Higher rate band: Savings (£2,000 – £500 personal savings allowance)	1,500 @ 40%		600
			31,220

continued overleaf

Tax liability		
Less: tax relieved on EIS investment	75,000 @ 30%	(22,500)
Less: tax deducted at source		
PAYE		(10,420)
Tax repayable		(1,700)

Note:
1. Personal allowance is not restricted as net adjusted income is £112,500. That is, £100,000 + grossed up personal pension of £10,000 + grossed up gift aid donation of £2,500.

NIC Calculation

Class 1 primary NIC (paid by employee on earnings from employment, but not on BIK, at 12% and 2%) = (upper earnings limit − earnings threshold) @ 12%.

$$£$$

$$£43,000 \ - \ £8,060 \ = £34,940 @ 12\% = \ 4,192.80$$
$$£105,000 - £43,000 = £62,000 @ 2\% \ = \ \underline{1,240.00}$$
$$5,432.80$$

As Mike is a company director, it is his annual earnings that are considered when assessing his NIC contributions (regardless of whether he is paid on a weekly or monthly basis).

Class 1 secondary NIC (paid by employers on earnings from employment @ 13.8%).
$$£105,000 \ - \ £8,112 \ = \ £96,888 @ 13.8\% = \ £13,370.54$$

Class 1A NIC (paid by employers on BIK @ 13.8%) £10,200 @ 13.8% = £1,407.60

Task 21 Solution

To: Martina Smithers

Subject: Briefing note – preparation of MCL directors' income tax returns

MCL has negotiated a fee with Shield Kenwick to prepare the income tax computations of the directors each year for a small fixed fee of £500. Any additional advice sought or work done for directors will be charged at normal rates to the director concerned.

By doing this, independence is established from your employers and any information provided by you or any of the directors to enable us to complete their income tax returns is not disclosed to MCL or any other director.

For convenience, MCL will provide confidential payroll and benefits information to us. Our tax manager will issue an engagement letter confirming the full details of our appointment, which you should read carefully and, if you are in agreement, sign and return.

Task 22 Solution

To: Martina Smithers

Subject: Briefing Note – residency and domicile rules

The extent to which you or your partner will be taxed in the UK on your worldwide income depends on your:

- residence; and
- domicile status.

Your income tax status

To determine how much of your worldwide income will be taxed in the UK, we have to look at each criterion separately.

Residence

The statutory residence test (SRT) is used to determine if an individual is UK resident or not. The SRT has three key components:

1. an automatic overseas test;
2. an automatic UK test; and
3. a sufficient ties test.

Each of the three components has several tests and each test requires a number of conditions to be met.

- If any of the automatic overseas tests apply to an individual, they are not UK resident for the tax year in question.
- If none of the automatic overseas tests apply, someone is automatically UK resident if at least one of the automatic UK tests applies. An individual is also UK resident if none of the automatic overseas tests and none of the automatic UK tests apply, but they have sufficient UK ties for the tax year. These include ties such as family, accommodation and work connections.

It is therefore necessary to work through the tests systematically in order to determine whether an individual is resident in the UK.

If you leave or come to the UK partway through the tax year, the tax year may be split (provided your circumstances meet the specific conditions required). This will mean that you pay tax only from the period you are resident in the UK, rather than the whole of the tax year. Split-year treatment applies to individuals coming to the UK to work or live, subject to meeting certain conditions.

As you joined MCL on 6 April 2017 and will spend 183 days or more in the UK, you will meet the first of the automatic UK tests under the SRT and will therefore be treated as UK resident for the 2017/18 tax year.

Domicile

Domicile is a matter of general law, not tax law.

Domicile is distinct from residence, i.e. one can be resident in more than one country, but domiciled in only one country. There are three types of domicile relevant to income and capital gains tax.

Domicile of origin is acquired at birth. This is normally the domicile of that individual's father. This is an individual's original domicile and can be very difficult to lose.

Domicile can change if a person acquires a different domicile of dependence or domicile of choice. **Domicile of dependence** is acquired if the father's domicile changes while an individual is under 16 years old. To acquire **domicile of choice**, a person must change domicile by severing ties with the old country and establishing a permanent life in the new country.

You would therefore be UK domiciled, as you were born in the UK and never made a determined decision to move your domicile to France.

Resident and domiciled

Such an individual is liable to UK income tax on his worldwide personal income and gains on an arising basis, irrespective of where it is earned and whether or not it is remitted to the UK.

Resident but not domiciled

An individual who is resident but not domiciled in the UK (e.g. a citizen of the United States working in the UK) has the choice of whether to use the arising basis of taxation to account for worldwide income and gains or the remittance basis (i.e. paying tax on income and gains accruing in the UK, but paying tax on foreign income and gains as they are remitted to the UK). Access to the remittance basis of taxation is not automatic and depends on how much foreign income and gains you have earned.

There are special rules for employment earnings, which are dealt with below.

Non-resident

An individual who is not resident in the UK is liable to UK income tax on UK income arising in the UK. Non-residents have no UK liability on overseas income. In general, a non-resident individual is not entitled to allowances (such as personal allowances, blind person's allowances, married couple's allowances, age allowances and so on). However, citizens of the European Economic Area are entitled despite being non-resident, which is of relevance to Paul.

As a result, for 2017/18 and beyond it is likely that you will be taxed in the UK on your worldwide income (as you will be resident and domiciled in the UK), which will include:

- UK salary and Vodafone dividend plus any other income you may have arising in Ireland or the UK;
- French rental income;
- French deposit interest.

Arising basis

A person who is resident in the UK is normally taxed on the arising basis. This means that the taxpayer will pay tax on all of his income as it arises and on gains as they accrue.

Remittance basis

Remittance basis means that you only account for UK tax on foreign income and/or gains when you bring them into the UK. You can only choose to use the remittance basis of taxation if you are resident in the UK during a tax year, you are not domiciled in the UK and you have foreign income/gains during the year you are resident in the UK.

Even if you are eligible to use the remittance basis, it does not mean that you have to use the remittance basis. The taxpayer might decide instead to pay UK tax on his worldwide income and/or gains on an arising basis and claim relief from UK tax on foreign tax that he must also pay.

If the taxpayer decides to use the remittance basis, the taxpayer may have to make a claim to use the remittance basis. If you have £2,000 or more unremitted foreign income and/or gains arising in the relevant tax year and you want to use the remittance basis, you must make a claim. (If you have less than £2,000 unremitted foreign income and/or gains, you can use the remittance basis without making a claim.)

Please note that if you have been resident in the UK for seven out of the past nine tax years, you have to pay a remittance basis charge of £30,000 if you make the claim to use the remittance basis. This annual charge is increased to £60,000 if resident in the UK for 12 out of the past 14 tax years; and to £90,000 if resident in the UK for 17 out of the past 20 tax years. In addition, if the remittance basis has been claimed, you will not be entitled to any personal allowances.

Task 23 Solution

To: Martina Smithers

Subject: Projected income tax return 2017/18 with notes

To complete the income tax computation, we need to look at your income sources very closely to ascertain how much to include.

Verizon LLC dividend – arises in the USA and is paid without deduction of UK tax. The Irish tax paid is added back. Under double taxation provisions, relief is available for the lower of the USA and UK taxes – see income tax computation.

	£
Gross dividend	3,750
Less: US tax deducted	562.50
Net received	3,187.50

Rents from your French chalet – from a tax perspective, you will be subject to UK income tax on your share.

Deposit in Banque Paribas (France) – you will be liable to income tax on any interest credited to this account in 2017/18.

For the calculation, I estimate that the account will be transferred in October 2017. I have also assumed there is no French tax deducted. You might let me know if this is not the case.

Deposit balance £300,000 @ 4% pa half share of the interest = £6,000.

Your salary and benefits arise in the UK and therefore are fully taxable as follows:

	£	
Salary for year	70,000.00	
BIK – Car	12,950.00	for year
BIK – Golf club	1,200.00	for year
BIK – Accommodation	1,900.00	for year
Gross earnings	86,050.00	

You may deduct the entire amount of your pension contribution of £2,800.

Martina Smithers

Income tax computation projected for 2017/18 (based on 2016/17 rates and allowances)

	Non-savings	Savings	Dividends	Total
	£	£	£	£
Employment income				
Salary	70,000			70,000
Benefits in kind	16,050			16,050
Less: pension contributions (£70,000 × 0.04)	(2,800)			(2,800)
	83,250			83,250
Bank deposit interest		6,000		6,000
Dividends			3,750	3,750
Rental income (£11,800/2)	5,900			5,900
Net income	89,150	6,000	3,750	98,900
Less: personal allowance	(11,000)			(11,000)
Taxable income	78,150	6,000	3,750	87,900

		£
Income tax due:		
Basic rate band: Non-savings	£32,000.00 @ 20%	6,400.00
Higher rate band: Non-savings	£46,150.00 @ 40%	18,460.00
Higher rate band: Savings	£500.00 @ 0% (Note 1)	0.00
	£5,500.00 @ 40%	2,200.00
Higher rate band: Dividends (£5,000 dividend allowance)	£3,750.00 @ 0%	0.00
	£87,900.00	
Tax liability		27,060.00
Less: dividend tax withheld at source (Note 2)		(0.00)
Tax payable		27,060.00

Note:
1. Personal savings allowance.
2. Martina is not given a tax credit for the French savings account as the question did not state tax was deducted at source.

The amount of double tax relief on the US dividend is capped at the lower of:

- the foreign tax on the dividend (i.e. £562.50); or
- the UK tax that would be suffered on that foreign dividend (see below).

The UK liability on the income is calculated by treating the foreign income as the top level of the individual's income in their tax return and comparing what the total tax liability (including all other sources of income) is with the foreign income included, and then what the tax liability is with the foreign income ignored. The difference between the two is the amount of UK tax that would be suffered on the foreign income.

In the calculation above, the UK tax on the foreign dividends is nil as the dividend allowance of £5,000 covers the amount of dividends received. As the foreign tax (£562.50) is higher than the UK tax suffered (which was nil), no double tax relief is available.

You will also have a liability to NIC under Class 1. The NIC calculation is as follows:

	£
£8,060 @ 0%	0
£34,940 (£43,000 – £8,060) @ 12%	4,192.80
£27,000 (£70,000 – £43,000) @ 2%	540.00
	4,732.80

Income tax return payment and filing obligations in the UK
If the correct tax has been collected under PAYE or by deduction at source and no further tax is chargeable, then no income tax return need be filed for that tax year. If a taxpayer has to file a tax return for any tax year, he can choose to file a paper return or file online. A paper return must be submitted by the **later** of:

- 31 October following the tax year; and
- three months after it is issued.

A four-page short tax return (STR) is available for taxpayers with simpler tax affairs.

An online return must be submitted by 31 January following the tax year.

Tax not collected through PAYE or by other deduction at source must be paid by 31 January following the tax year.

Payments on account are required by certain taxpayers – most likely those in self-employment. These payments on account are due on 31 January in the tax year and on 31 July immediately after the end of the tax year. Each payment on account is 50% of prior tax year's income tax and Class 4 NICs, less tax suffered at source. This is called the relevant amount. Payments on account should not apply here as the exceptions to payments on account will likely apply, i.e. payments on account are not required if:

- the relevant amount is less than £1,000; or
- more than 80% of the income tax liability for the previous year was met by deduction at source.

The second of these should apply in your case. Also, if you believe that your income tax liability for any period will be lower than the required payments on account, you can apply to reduce the payments on account to the actual liability.

Interest can arise in respect of all payments not made by the due date.

An additional penalty can be levied on late balancing payments. If a balancing payment is more than 30 days late, a 5% penalty on the late tax will be levied. A further 5% penalty can be levied if the balancing payment is more than six months late and 12 months late. Penalties must be paid within 30 days of imposition – otherwise interest will accrue on the penalty from the date payment is due, i.e. 30 days of imposition.

A fixed penalty of £100 is levied on the late filing of a tax return. Additional daily penalties of £10 per day may be levied in respect of returns that are more than three months late. The daily penalty can be imposed for a maximum of 90 days. If the delay is more than six months after the filing date, the penalty will be the greater of £300 and 5% of the liability. These penalties may be set aside if a reasonable excuse is forwarded (though these are limited in scope). Failure to submit the return after 12 months will result in a penalty – the greater of £300 and 5% of the liability.

In respect of an incorrect return submitted fraudulently or negligently, then a tax-geared penalty of up to 100% of tax that would have been lost may be levied.

Task 24 Solution

To: Paul

Subject: Projected income tax return 2017/18 with notes

In order to determine how much of your worldwide income will be taxed in the UK, we must look at each criteria separately.

Residence – UK

Prior to 2017/18, you only spent two weeks' holiday in the UK. In 2017/18, you will spend 114 days (i.e. 50 × 2-day weekends plus two weeks' vacation).

We need to work through each of the three components of the statutory residence test (SRT) to determine your residency position for the 2017/18 tax year.

1. Automatic Overseas Test
    The only tests that may be relevant to you under the automatic overseas test are the second and third tests:

    (a) Second test: **the individual was resident in the UK for none of the preceding three tax years and spends fewer than 46 days in the UK in the relevant tax year**.
        As you were resident in the UK for more than 46 days you do not meet this test.
    (b) Third test: **the individual works "sufficient hours" overseas for the tax year without any significant breaks from that overseas work and during that tax year:**
        (i) **has fewer than 31 UK work days (a UK work day is a day where they do more than three hours work in the UK)**; and
        (ii) **the individual spends fewer than 91 days (excluding deemed days) in total in the UK.**

    While it is likely that you will meet the "sufficient hours" element of the test and also have fewer than 31 work days in the UK, as you do not spend fewer than 91 days in the UK in total this test is not met.

2. Automatic UK Test
    Next, we check if you meet any of the automatic UK tests. None of these tests apply – you are not in the UK for 183 days or more, you have a home in the Republic of Ireland and stay there for more than 30 days (which precludes you satisfying the second automatic UK test) and you do not work in the UK so would not meet the third automatic UK test.

3. Sufficient Ties Test
    As your residency position is not conclusive under either the automatic overseas tests or the automatic UK tests, we must assess whether you have sufficient UK ties, together with the number of days you spend in the UK, to be treated as UK resident.
    As you spend 114 days in the UK and were not UK resident in any of the previous three tax years, you must have at least three UK ties to be treated as UK resident.

The ties are as follows:

(a) Family tie – is met as your wife, Martina, and children would be UK resident in the 2017/18 tax year;

(b) Accommodation tie – is met as your family home is in the UK;

(c) Work tie – not met;

(d) 90-day tie – not relevant (as you did not spend more than 90 days in the UK in either of the two previous tax years);

(e) Country tie – not relevant as you were not resident for one of the three previous tax years (in any case, you spend more time in the Republic of Ireland).

Since you have only two UK ties in the 2017/18 tax year, you will be considered as non-UK resident under the SRT.

Domicile – UK

As your family is from Dublin and you have not 'cut your ties' there, you are ROI domiciled.

So long as you remain UK non-resident, you will only be liable to UK income tax on income arising in the UK, i.e. the rent from your holiday home in Essex.

Your projected income tax computation for 2017/18 is given below.

Income tax computation projected for 2017/18 (based on 2016/17 rates and allowances)

		£
Rental income		8,000
Less: Personal allowance (£11,000 available)		(8,000)
Taxable income		Nil
Income tax due:		
Basic rate band	Nil @ 20%	Nil

As you are a non-resident landlord, your tenant will need to deduct 20% tax at source from rental payments made to you, unless you receive clearance from HMRC to receive these rental payments without deduction of withholding taxes and also provides a copy of this clearance to the tenant. Any tax deducted at source can be set against your income tax liability when you file your income tax return and a repayment received, if due. In this example, it is assumed that you have received clearance to receive rents without deduction at source.

Income tax return payment and filing obligations in the UK

As you have UK-sourced income, you have self-assessment obligations. You will need to submit an online tax return by 31 January following the tax year to avoid interest and penalties. Shield Kenwick can prepare all the necessary paperwork upon receiving appropriate instructions from you well in advance of this deadline.

Finally, I would be extremely concerned that you bring your income tax affairs in this country up to date. Penalties for a late or incorrect submission of a tax return are detailed above. In particular, you should apply for clearance from HMRC to receive the rental income without deduction of tax at source.

Your income tax position will change when you come to live in the UK permanently, and it is likely you will be treated as UK resident (but potentially still non-domiciled).

You will then be liable to UK income tax on:

▦ income arising in the UK; and
▦ income outside of the UK depending on the amount remitted into the UK. (Please see previous notes on remitted income.)

Task 25 Solution

MEMO

To:	**Michael Smithers**
From:	**Chris, Shield Kenwick**
Date:	**26 January 2018**
Re:	**VAT Return, October–December 2017**

VAT on purchases

Following a review, there are a number of adjustments to be made to VAT on purchases.

1. Petty cash, as there is no invoice the VAT may not be reclaimed – a credit entry is made to the VAT account.
2. You may not recover duty paid on the import of plant from the USA and need to journal the amount of £250 to the Plant account. The VAT amount is included in the amended VAT on purchases report.
3. The posting of M. Wiley Ltd is correct with regard to VAT on purchases. Under the reverse charge procedures, the VAT must also be added to the VAT on sales report and credited to the VAT account.
   No reverse charge was made in respect of Weave Magic GmbH, a German supplier. VAT at 20% must be accounted for on sales and the purchase – this must be adjusted for in the VAT on sales and purchases report and in the VAT account.
4. MCL may include the VAT on this SAD document in its October–December 2017 VAT return.

The adjustments to the VAT on sales are:
   VAT should have been charged on the sale to Marshia Joan at 20%, as no VAT number is available.
   The corrected VAT on purchases, VAT on sales and VAT reconciliation are as follows:

VAT on purchases amended October–December 2017

		Net	VAT
		£	**£**
		150,761.21	19,217.08
12 Nov 2017	Dryers America Inc. – Plant	2,900.00	2,900.00
8 Dec 2017	Weave Magic GmbH – Machine repairs		210.00
19 Nov 2017	Materials Unlimited Inc. – USA		230.76
			22,557.84

VAT on sales amended October–December 2017

		Net	VAT
		£	£
		175,400.00	1,501.50
11 Nov 2017	M. Wiley – Plant		2,660.00
8 Dec 2017	Weave Magic GmbH – Machine repairs		210.00
7 Nov 2017	Marshia Joan	404.93	80.99
10 Dec 2017	Phillipa Treacy	300.00	
			4,452.49

My Company Ltd – VAT account amended from 1 October–31 December 2017

		DR	CR
		£	£
31 Dec 2017	Closing Balance	21,080.46	
6 Nov 2017	Petty Cash		214.88
11 Nov 2017	M. Wiley – Plant		2,660.00
12 Nov 2017	Dryers America Inc. – Plant		250.00
8 Dec 2017	Weave Magic GmbH – Machine repairs	210.00	
8 Dec 2017	Weave Magic GmbH – Machine repairs		210.00
7 Nov 2017	Marshia Joan		80.99
19 Nov 2017	Materials Unlimited Inc. – USA	230.76	
	Revised closing balance		18,105.35
		21,521.22	21,521.22

Task 26 Solution

Briefing Note: Intrastat and EC Sales Lists

Intrastat

If you are a VAT-registered business and you sell or move goods to other VAT-registered businesses within the European Union (EU), you must record and report data on your activities.

There are two systems – Intrastat and the European Community (EC) Sales List.

An Intrastat return is the means for collecting statistics on the trade in goods (services are excluded) within the EU and is known as a Supplementary Statistical Declaration (SSD).

The threshold is £1,500,000 pa for arrivals and £250,000 pa for dispatches. For UK businesses selling goods and services to other Member States that are below this level, only a statistical return, known as the EC Sales List, is required to be completed.

All VAT-registered businesses that have supplied goods or services to or acquired goods or services from another EU Member State must complete Box 8 or 9 of their VAT return.

For Intrastat, if the value exceeds a legally set threshold – currently £1,500,000 for arrivals and £250,000 for dispatches – businesses must also provide more detailed information in Supplementary Declarations.

All VAT-registered businesses which supply goods to other VAT-registered businesses in the EU must also provide details of the transactions on the EC Sales List.

Intrastat covers any goods that move between the UK and any other EU country by way of trade. This includes a supply of goods that are:

▓ bought or sold;
▓ transferred between divisions of a company in different EU Member States;
▓ sent for process or returned afterwards;
▓ to be installed or used in construction; or
▓ on long-term hire or lease.

Intrastat is designed to build a picture of trading patterns and values within the EU. The results are used to create essential data on the UK's trading and balance of payments data, which cannot be created in any other way.

Since 1 January 2010, you must report the value of any services you may buy or sell from businesses in other EU Member States. If you supply or receive goods as part of a service contract (e.g. if you sell cleaning equipment as part of a contract to clean offices), the value of the equipment sold must be recorded.

If the value of the goods or services you buy from suppliers, or sell to customers, in other EU Member States (referred to as 'arrivals' and 'dispatches' respectively) exceeds the annual threshold, you will need to supply the relevant Supplementary Declarations (SDs). These provisions apply separately to arrivals and dispatches. Therefore, if a business exceeds the threshold for arrival of goods, but not dispatches, it only has to complete SDs for arrivals.

The threshold applies on a calendar year basis, running from January to December. If you are not required to provide SDs at the beginning of the year, you must monitor the position and if, at the end of any month, the value of dispatches or arrivals in the calendar year has exceeded the threshold, you must submit SDs on a monthly basis for the rest of the year.

You only need to report the value of the goods that count as arrivals or dispatches. You do not need to report any excise duty. In most cases, this means that you will record the invoice or contract price of the goods.

You do not need to report goods that are:

▓ moved temporarily with no change of ownership;
▓ not moved for trade purposes;
▓ goods in transit through the UK; or
▓ goods sent for or returned after repair.

There are specific details required on the SDs. You'll need to provide:

▓ your VAT registration details, branch ID (if applicable) and business name and address;
▓ VAT-registration details, branch ID (if applicable) and name and address of any agent you use;
▓ the period covered by the SD;
▓ number of lines completed on the SD;
▓ the value of the goods (in Sterling);
▓ a nature of transaction code to indicate the type of transaction;
▓ the country code to indicate where the goods have been supplied to or received from;
▓ delivery terms (only mandatory for traders whose EU trade exceeds the delivery term threshold – £24 million from 1 January 2014);
▓ the commodity code of the goods; and
▓ the net mass (in kilograms) or supplementary unit. You will need to find the commodity code to determine the unit you use.

You must keep specific records to comply with your Intrastat and SD responsibilities. You must:

- keep a copy of each SD you or your agent makes;
- retain all papers and documents that have been used to compile the SD;
- produce the records to HMRC when required; and
- keep the records for at least six years.

You must classify the goods on the SD using the appropriate commodity code in the Intrastat Classification Nomenclature (ICN). This system shows what type of product you are referring to by using eight-digit codes, set up in four pairs of two digits. As the code progresses, greater detail about the product is shown by each pair of digits.

Reconciling SDs and VAT returns

The figures you declare on your SDs should agree with the totals on your VAT return. However, there are circumstances where the figures may differ. There are processes you can follow that will help you save management time and avoid you having to deal with queries from HMRC.

There are times when the values you declare on Box 8 or 9 on your VAT return will differ from the values declared on your SDs due to the different reporting requirements of the two systems. These include:

- goods sent for or returned after processing;
- sales to private individuals;
- returned goods; and
- credit notes.

European Community (EC) Sales List

If you are registered for VAT and you supply goods to businesses **registered for VAT** in other EU Member States, you must provide details of these sales on an EC Sales List (ESL). Since 1 January 2010, you are also required to report cross-border sales of services.

The information provided is used by the UK and other EU Member States to make sure that VAT has been accounted for correctly.

You must supply:

- your VAT registration number and address details;
- the country code relevant to your customer's location;
- your customer's VAT registration number;
- the total value of the goods supplied; and
- where appropriate, indicate if you are an intermediary supplier in a triangular transaction (this is a transaction in which a trader in one EU country is an intermediary between a supplier in a second EU country, and the final customer in a third EU country).

You must provide an ESL on a calendar quarterly basis; although in some circumstances you can complete it monthly or annually. In any case, the ESL must be submitted no later than 21 days from the end of the reporting period for online submissions, and 14 days from the end of the period for paper submissions.

There are four ways you can submit data to the ESL:

- via an internet service using either the online form or the bulk upload facility;
- via a new XML channel, using either a commercial software package or a bespoke program;

- via electronic data interchange (EDI) using the EDIFACT standard; or
- a paper form.

You should include the total value of supplies to your customer. This includes the price of the goods, along with any related services – such as freight and transport charges – which form part of the invoice price. You must then round down the figures to the nearest £ Sterling. If you have made more than one sale to a customer in the period, you should add the sales together and report one total.

If you do not make any sales to VAT-registered businesses in other EU countries within the reporting period, you do not need to submit an ESL.